Bodywearers

by Connie Colwell Miller

Published by Sol Books,
an imprint of Skywater Publishing Company,
Minneapolis, Minnesota.
www.solbooks.com

Copyright © 2008 Skywater Publishing Company

All rights reserved. No part of this publication
may be reproduced in whole or in part
without written permission of the publisher.

Acknowledgements

The author and publisher wish to express their grateful appreciation to the following publications in which earlier versions of these poems first appeared: "The Bodywearers", *Applauze Magazine*; "From the Basement Apartment of a Young Poet", *Minnesota River Review*; "How They Try to Sleep on a Bed That Is Too Small" and "My Father", *Mankato Poetry Review*

Library of Congress Cataloging-in-Publication Data
Miller, Connie Colwell, 1976–
   Bodywearers / by Connie Colwell Miller.
   p. cm. — (Upper Midwest Writers Series)
   ISBN 978-0-9793081-1-6 (paperback)
   ISBN 978-0-9793081-4-7 (e-book)
   I. Title.
PS3613.I5334B63 2008
811'.6—dc22   2007027675

Photo Credits
Shutterstock, interior flourishes; Shutterstock/Bocos Benedict, cover (green background); Shutterstock/Vansina Natalia, cover (stomach)

To my husband and my kids
for being the stuff that's better than poetry.

Table of Contents

The Bodywearers 7

The Wearing
Willow, Stove 13
Joseph's Real Indian Stuff 14
From the Basement Apartment
    of a Young Poet 15
Of Bedsheets and Underwear 16
The Distance Between 17
The Heartbreak of Fatherhood 18
In Loving Remorse 20
The Things I Do 21
Nudes, Reclined 22
The Tracheotomy. 23
Our Mothers in the Other World 24
How They Try to Sleep on a Bed
    That Is Too Small 25
Old Hat 26
A View of the Night Sky
    from Duluth, Minnesota 28
Pike's Place, Downtown Seattle:
    The Last Stop 30

Weaknesses 32
A Boy's Life. 34
The Best Words I Can Find 36

Of The Body
Living This Land 41
The Red-Tail on the Minnesota 42
There Is Something I Hear 43
Thanatophobia 44
I-94 Westbound through Minnesota 45
The Sweet Spot 46
My Father 47
Starting Fire in the Redwoods 50
Pine Bed on the Bank of the Baptism 51
A Poem for the Unborn. 52
My Mother's Ring. 53
Life 54
Milk 56
Loss. 58
The Heron. 59
The Road Trip 60

The Bodywearers

I think we have forgotten
why we wear our bodies.
We drag them from our beds
each morning and consider:
I am blonde. I am large.
I am scaly and yellow.

Look down. See the body
among the pillows? That
is not you, though you wear
it. See those hips and the knee jutting out
and the stem of that sex?
Neither is that you. Your body
contains you, a mite of sand
in the tongue of a clam.

Look there: a woman Titian
would have painted in long, lusty strokes,
dying for the figure of a waif.
Or there: the white girl who came of age
inside her Asian body.
Or this fragile man
in his huge man's case. We all
have this — this approximate us.

Bodywearers

Stop it. You wear your body
because the wasp stings and
because the pebble wedges hard
between your nail and
the flesh of your toe. You
wear it to smell your lover's
hot breath and the skunk's
potent, unbearable stuff. To taste
the sweat in the valley between
her breasts, the bitter blade
of grass, the sourmilk musk
your daughter breathes. And to hear
the winter-stiff pines bristle in wind.

I say to you: Look at the pock
on my forehead. I am looking
at your small breasts, your blue
and nerveless tooth. And I am
throwing your body away. I will
strip myself to the core
for you. Or I can wear myself
the wrong way out. See the mole
on my back? I see the dappled flab
at your middle. We are what we are,
bodywearers only. So lay your body
over mine and use it. Use it and use it
until our souls spark like flints.

The Wearing

Willow Stove
— *after Beckian Fritz Goldberg*

My father was a willow. My mother was a
stove. Weathered, he bowed loosely toward
my upturned face, tickled my cheek, and re-stood.

She, stocked around the middle, and small,
used iron hands to untie knots and open
every coin purse. Rarely, he'd pull her

toward him and press his lips on hers
for show, and she'd tear away, bubbling
with anger. The floorboards creaked

from so much weighty pacing. Then, he'd
stand at the screen and love the storms, green his face
by the damp moonlight. She'd stir

potatoes at the stovetop, her slipper tapping
the dog bowl, and their fierce combustion — my life.

Joseph's Real Indian Stuff
— *Taos Pueblo, April 2001*

He pulls off an outdated pair of reading
glasses as I duck through the low adobe
doorway. He rises from behind the counter
like the moon. Long wrapped braids run over
the squares of his shoulders and halt
just above his enormous belly. He greets me
softly and not kindly: this is both home
and store. An earthen stove looms behind him.

I touch the fetishes with my fingertips,
the turquoise, the tiger's eye, the lined acoma pots.
He watches me, his glasses poised at
his side. His eyes are like thumbs on my
cheeks. I turn but they press against my back.

There is no noise louder than this
Pueblo silence. Even the dogs here do not
bark. I can bear it no longer.

As I leave, I turn to him, "Thank you."
But my words mend nothing: not this
soul-deep intrusion, not white fingers
playing over blood red clay. Not being large
nor being poor, not even the energy
lost in the simple act of enduring. Joseph
grunts and comes to life again, replaces his
glasses. Sits to work his crossword.

From the Basement Apartment of a Young Poet

I am reading, like always. Or, no,
I am sitting, arms raised in an M
behind my head. I am thinking
about reading. Poetry is maturity,
they tell me. It will come with age

and wisdom and learning to see
meaning in a patch of clover
over grass and a set of empty
swings. For the sake of the poem,
I should be outside, skitting

my toenails across the loose
grit of my driveway. But
I am sitting on my bed and
listening to the steady squeak of a bird
and the hum of the AC. There

is no meaning here, and if there is,
I will only see it later, around age
forty, they say. So I will read and fall
in love and be burned and
live more and come back here, and

I will see the scab of clover,
the smile of swing, and remember
how it meant loneliness, a green
summer in an empty room, and
a window-well, uterine, waiting for rain.

Of Bedsheets and Underwear

Morning enters, and I ease
soft into consciousness (the reel
of a dream claps its endfilm lightly
on the wheel). My lover's day
has begun. I sense it in the cool
freedom at my back and shoulder.
I pull the comforter close and breathe
him deeply in. I love this smell of male,
like fists of earth. Sour, private,
embarrassing (caught sniffing the blotch
of juice staining my panties).
This is his body's fragrance: sweat
and wear, heat and secretion. I open
my eyes and see more of it on the floor
beside my bed: his underwear, discarded, unfresh,
soft with wear and molded to the tender curve
of ass and cock, and (most perfect of all)
a dark stain in the boyish cups of cloth
that this grown man wears every day like skin.

The Distance Between

Today, you're tired of your lover's
hands. Of the way his touch bristles
the fine hair about your nipples. Tired

of your body and its arching need
to meet those hands. You're sick of your
idiot heart, straining at its box. Of

the quickening pulse beneath your
wrist when his lips part or his brows
crease in orgasm. Even your panties are tired

of their bureau and want to be pulled
out and dropped crotch-up on the carpeting,
stains and all. Most of all, you're tired

of remembering how he lay there
with your blood smeared up
his thighs like clay, thinking idly

of something so beautiful
that you were bored to tears.

Bodywearers

The Heartbreak of Fatherhood

Evenings, you park your rig out back
and step indoors to wash the road
from your hands and face. These nights
you will be Daddy, the gruff figure your
daughter waits for beneath the dim kitchen
light. She is fresh from the bath, and to her
you smell of man, rough skin, and your
breath is warm on her nape before bedtime.

You, a man who has steered truck down 94
with only your knee, are also the man
who will feel the fine curve of your daughter's
buttocks as she sits on your thigh for storytime.
There is something about the way she tugs
absently at the edges of your fingernails. You
button a tiny button across the white down
of her spine, pull tight a purple ribbon
around a tail of fine hair. You will refasten
a bandage to a knee no thicker than your own
coarse wrist.

Then one day, beneath her tee, you will notice
the breasts, swollen and magnificent as grapefruit.
She will begin to walk, carried by the wide basin
of a woman's sturdy hips. She looks at you,
as through your own coal-black eyes, and the look
nearly strikes you down. And she says,

"You just don't understand. I'm not as pretty
as the other girls," and you — father, lover, child,
and man — will think, *Her button, her hair, the amazing
flesh of her bottom, oh, this cruel and unjust world.*

In Loving Remorse

I know what people say
about saving yourself for marriage.
I know how the hymen should burst
in consummation and how bastards
are made and then, haplessly,
born. I've heard the tight-lipped warnings
about the users, the players, the men
who want pussy, the men who invariably
"think with the wrong heads." And,
as it happened, you and I did not marry.
Nor did I marry the man before you or the man
before him. But I do not regret the love
we made, not in the hotel shower in Rapid
City, nor on the floor of my college dorm,
nor on the flat rock in the middle of the river.
Rather, I think, my love gets better
with each making. With each thrust, each
arch, each spiral toward madness. These
acts of love are not what I regret, not
the things I wish I'd saved for marriage.
I regret the words, those coins of love,
that never mean the same thing twice.

The Things I Do

Outside leaves blow crisp as husks.
If you were here I'd say,

It sounds like tide out there. Instead,
I snap pillows into cases, scour both

toilet bowl and check-tiled floor.
I curl my toes and make other quiet

movements you don't
see. Some things I cross off lists.

I think I yawn. Once or twice I lick
a finger, place a stamp, sneeze.

Afternoon arrives, same as where you are,
and I think you check your fridge,

drink from the spigot, grip the faucet long.
I think I see you square your shoulders

in the latticed noon-light, watch the wind clap
leaves together, and between them, small
    brown birds.

Nudes Reclined

You are sleeping,
nude, in the morning sun
when I remember
your words from the night
before, "It just feels
good to be touched
by somebody, I guess."

Now the sun outlines
your shoulder, jaw,
ear, and arch of nose. Your lips
are puffed in sleep, lashes
like fat caterpillars
curled on each lid,
beads of mucous
in the corners where bits
of dream seep out.
Several curls
on your sternum,
like the private hairs
in drains, then
farther, a smooth two-sided brush
meeting at the navel,
headed toward your sex.

And now I remember,
I said, "That's okay, too,
I guess."

The Tracheotomy

From downstairs come the wet rattles
of my father's cough. "Sleep tight,
Miss Muffet," he will come to say
before bed, with such a deep vibing
of the voicebox, as if I've lain my back
against the butt of a cello.

I remember the hole in Aunt Betty's throat
the size of a quarter. Through this,
she breathed. And before it healed,
she was smoking again, holding
a cigarette to the wound
as if to lips. To speak, she swallowed,
belched each syllable, a hideous,
toneless staccato.

But for him, I tell myself, there will
be no cancer, no hole rudely
knocked in his ruddy farmer's neck,
no removal of the trachea
from the body of the tracheate.
No, for my proud and callused
father, there must be no dying.

Our Mothers in the Other World

In the world behind this one, your mother,
eight-months pregnant, stands at the spin-rack
at Penney's, fingering a sweater in each swollen
hand. The first, a shade of black dubbed
"blake." The second, a green called "glen."
In that same world, my mother, also pregnant,
but nine years later, reclines on her bed. "I'll name
her Molly," she says to her father. "I had a cow
named Molly, Mary Margaret. Think about that."

You and I slip sometimes into this other world,
the world where your mother chose the second shirt,
where my mother for once did not listen to another. And
we become them: you are not you, and I am not me. We
can see it in the mirror, those strange days where the nose
looks a little less like yours than it did the day before,
the days you're sure you were meant for something better.

But our lives are shaped by our names, the real me
eventually tells the real you. In this life, we have become
poets, friends, both poor and irrevocably impractical.
You were not named for down-to-earth green. I was not
named for the peppy family cow. But we live our lives
some days, suspended, as though we wish we had been.

How They Try to Sleep on a Bed That Is Too Small

He cups himself
against her, hooks
his arm above her head,
and pins her there,
the first in a set of parenthesis,
her body like a group
of sighing letters — a Y
where her shoulder meets
her neck and runs on toward her
chest, a P where the pink underbelly
of her left foot rests
on the knee of her right,
a V at the crook of her arm
as it bends idly across her frame.
His eyes open to the back
of her head, and his right ear,
pricked to attention, strains
to hear words escape the lazy O
of her mouth. But she is,
as the sheets beneath
them, bare and white, silent
in punctuated
sleep.

Old Hat

Sometimes we say nothing
over breakfast. Or we sit

in different rooms, reading
the same novel. Other times,

you scoot past me in the bathroom,
naked, and I am wet and clad

in towel. I bend over
the sink to spit.

No kiss or touch. These
are the times our orbits do not cross,

we revolve with different sides of face
to the sun. Like tonight, I hold

your hand movie-long, but it is not like
those first times, fingers laced, our blood

pulsing, mine, then yours, then mine,
and yours again. Somehow our bodies

have found their lives, they have crawled
back inside the mollusked shells, and we

Connie Colwell Miller

have begun to remember those things
which love so deftly shelled — the pile of bills,

the crumple of undone laundry,
the water-ring on the oak end table.

A View of the Night Sky from Duluth, Minnesota

Here is the place where, at each Monday's
unraveling, this family might leave twin
bins full of trash, or where, as clock hands
stretch toward summer's dusky curfew,

a boy might coast his seatless dirt bike
up the pebbled alley, over this grassy slope,
and into the yawning pool of porch light.
But now, this is the place where a young

couple sits, molding their spines into the boy's
moon-lit rub of lawn. See how they fingertip
the blades of grass and each other's shoe
lace tips? They are travelers here, miles from

home, and they like to think themselves lovers,
philosophers, even dreamers. Now see them
point and name constellations and watch them
blink, dizzy with human smallness. Here she

notes Cassiopeia, Ursa Major, he spots Scorpio,
all sparkling flecks of quartz on the curves of an
overturned bowl, and they think themselves
the spiders cupped beneath. Tomorrow they

will let birch trees sway like the masts of earth-
sunk ships, and there, behind that tree, she
will squat to pee, cupping her palm over
the flashlight beam so he will not see her,

primitive and vulnerable. He will become
head-heavy with beer until her laughter
swims in his ears and her face is cheek-shine
over the wavy heat of the campfire. But that is

tomorrow. Tonight they've yet to walk some
blocks back to the neon-rimmed motel, to close
their ears to the world and press against each
other until they feel the weight of their existence.

It will be there, beneath his hips, where now
there is nothing but the press of sky holding
him to earth. She will think how the stars here
winked their lies like a teasing grandfather.

The two will begin to feel, as they move into
one another that they are the only two who
exist, and they will whisper, until they believe,
that this is so.

Pike's Place, Downtown Seattle: The Last Stop

We walk to the marketplace and step
up the cobbles and under the loud lip
of awning. Our fingers are laced, the way
lovers show others they're lovers. The sun

stays leashed at the curb and, inside,
the dirty odor of produce. Fresh fish,
still wholly animal, lie coffinless in their
out-of-water graves. Little placards

like gravestones put forth their names
and worth, in ink. Metal spin-racks whine
with postcards, and a Korean man tells me
they are five for a dollar, plus tax.

We pass three large men, a shadowed trio
on a stoop, blues-ifying songs from the fifties.
The largest, one arm looped around a slender
pillar, stomps his foot like he's kickstarting

a bike. Tourists stand at long tables, appraising
T-shirts and aprons with a thumb-finger rub.
Locals buy fruit, loaves of fresh bread, maybe
a sprout of cut flowers if they're not in a hurry

to get somewhere else. You buy a pack of Juicy Fruit
from the man, who says thank you, and I
examine the underside of my hand, its clean flesh,
the soft pudge of the palm. You chew the stick

of gum and say you remember the taste as sweeter
and better when you chewed as a child. You do not
look at me as you speak this, but rather
watch the black man stomp and push sounds through

the loose O of his mouth. I am thinking of the walk
back and unmaking the bed as we do every night
at home and curling my thighs in sleep. I will keep
my fists close to my chest and the world I see

will be a film dropped between my eye and its lid.
We will allow our wounds to heal there, our dreams
licking them clean so we can start again tomorrow.

Weaknesses

Sometimes there is this
thing inside me, and I
eat white corn chips until

I need to unbutton the first
on my favorite pair of jeans.
Other times, I am bored or

lonely and go to listen to the
humming of my engine and drive
to the bookstore and buy, just

because I shouldn't. And there
are the times I bite my nails,
and the time I pick my scabs.

There are even times I rewrite
the pages in my address book
because I don't like the look

of Martin or Anderson or the
way I formed the 5 in Mother's
phone number. Sometimes I do

go out and have a drink and then
it's two, and by then, I'm dizzy,
but drinking is not one of my

Connie Colwell Miller

things. It is me who goes home,
by myself, after this night
when others sit stoned

and drunk, happy in alcoholic
bliss, and eats a tin of cashews,
or, not by myself, and has sex

without a condom. The morning
after our weakness is always the
same: we seem up to trying

it all again, at breakfast-time,
it is promising, with the sun
and some birds and sometimes warmth.

A Boy's Life

My husband and I are bathing
our son when, from among the suds
and tipping plastic boats and cups,
he finds his penis as it floats

limply between his thighs.
He grasps it and looks up at us,
his eyes dark and proud as palmed
pennies, and he calls it by name,

"Pee-pee." We laugh as parents laugh,
a wise pair of progenitors,
for we have taught our son his ABCs and
123s and reds and greens and blues.

He then points to the bulge of denim
at his father's crotch and says, "Daddy
pee-pee." And we laugh again to see
his neat cognition grinding out its data,

the folds of gray matter dividing and
deepening into themselves. But then,
it seems he suddenly forgets the warm
womb in which he floated, forgets that sack

of stickiness in which he learned to clench
his fist, to hiccup, to beat his terrible,
fearsome heart, he forgets the hard curve
of my bone as it pressed into his skull,

the pelvis and cervix spread wide for his exit.
He lifts his tender penis and says to us, "Mommy
no pee-pee." And I see my son's penis, so sexless,
so fragile, its folds and urine-dribbling tip, and I see

that he already holds it weapon-style
and strong, he is so very strong.

Bodywearers

The Best Words I Can Find

For me, it's like when you're driving
home for the holidays and you succumb
to the daydreams. You don't know how
it happens exactly, but
the roadside ditches fade, the engine
quiets, and you train the right-hand tire
to the line. At first you see the moments
ahead — the long oak table uncluttered at once,
six mismatched mugs of milk, a dog
beneath the legs of one chair. You see
your mother standing at the stove, your
father hunched in the doorway, blowing
cigarette smoke out the screen door.

Then you see yourself,
as only you can see you, and how
perfectly you fit among the objects
of this house. You can disappear
if you like, let your brother tell the jokes,
or you can draw
attention to yourself, shout so loud
the neighbors talk. But, instead, you think,
you will be good for once, stop snapping
at your brother, stop shoving the dog,
stop saying, I hate you, I hate you,
the crying.

Connie Colwell Miller

And then you are gone: you see
your own children birth themselves
through some unnamed canal,
and you must pick their names, work
for their food, and somehow — painfully —
love them.

When you snap out of this dream,
you are lost. The scenery
has changed. The last hill to St. Cloud
has passed. The woods, and
the sun-faded barn, but they
are not here. It's only Minnesota, and
you'll find your way back, but you'll
be late, you'll miss the moment your
mother finally turns to your father softly
and says, "I love you. I always have.
I'm a fool. And I love the world, the beautiful,
painful, living world."

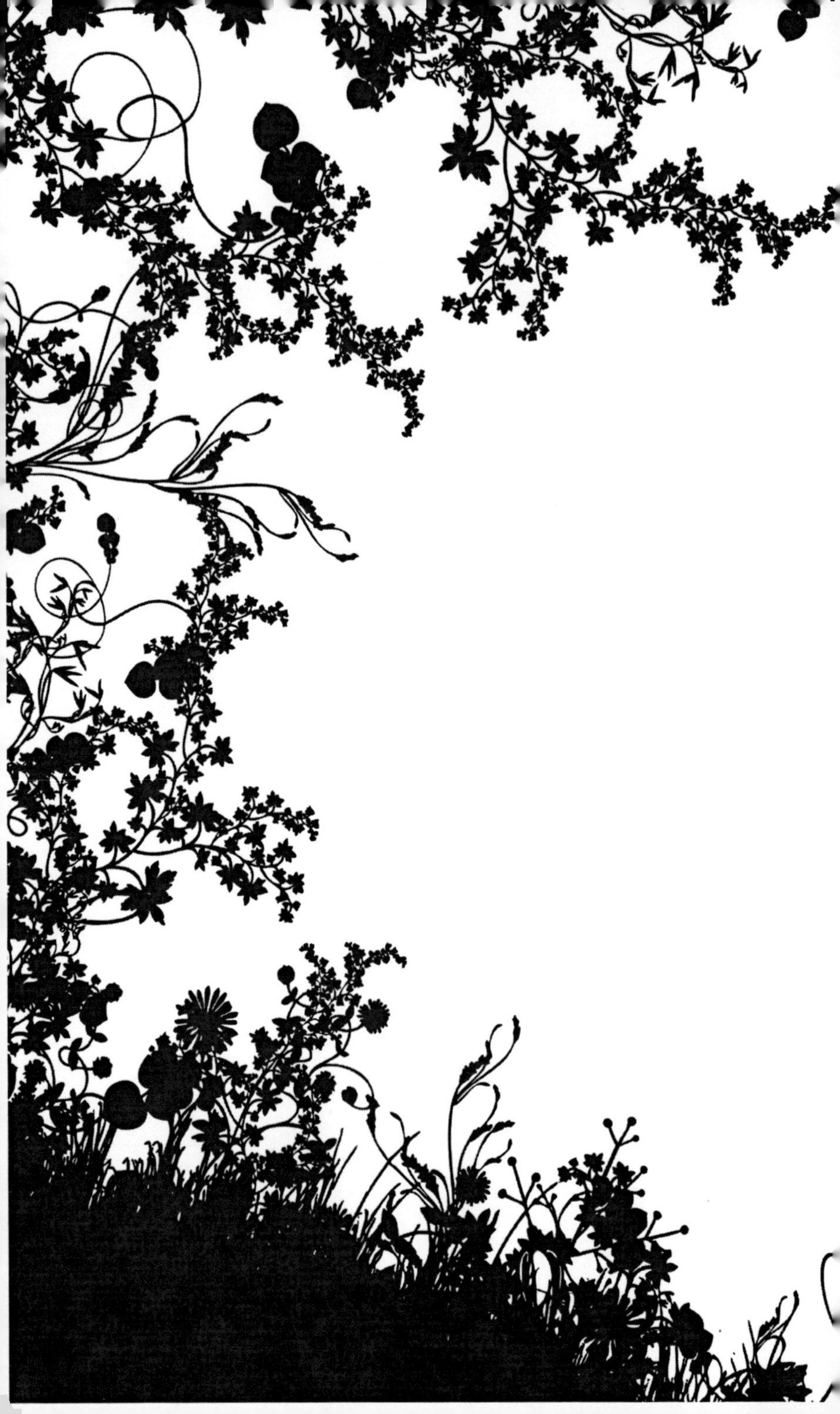

Of The Body

Living This Land

Driving the gravel home tonight,
I brake for possum.
I come to a complete
stop, surprised by this one's
carelessness, the needling
of his rat nose
toward the hot headlights,
and his stumbling, everywhere limbs.
I honk once to startle him back
to the ditch. Moments later,
in two leaping stones of light,
I recognize the eyes of a bounding
doe. I recall my husband's words: where
there's one, there's two. When I finally
hit the blacktop, the luminescent
white lines and yellow dashes
reassure me some. But then there's the
bat that beats its wings against my
windshield. And the milky frogs
that lunge at the wheel wells.
It's like a war out here.
I know inside my truck I'm nearly
invincible, but you can see how steadfast
I must be to defend my
right to be here.

The Red-Tail on the Minnesota

November, and the river
freezes between the two
breasts of Mankato. A hundred
crows near the banks, tossed
on the wind like loose ash over fire.

But the hawk, she is perched
on the arm of a bare deciduous,
steeling herself against the pelts
of ice. Her feathers pushed back
from her beak, her cere, her skull.
Under-feathers blow white as
snow, the wings blow rusty.

When she turns her head,
my breathing stops. She is living.
She scans the ground for mice or voles.

I have seen her light and leave
now twice. She seems always
perched and waiting.
There is patience here, I think,
like none I've ever seen. The hawk
on her frozen branch, talons rough
and reptilian, watching below
for the movement that will feed her.

There Is Something I Hear

when teeth bite crisp stalks
of celery, when boots

or doe hooves snap twigs in neat
halves, when a heft of snow

swooshes through thick arms of pine.
It is the ice clink in pink

lemonade, it is a sunflower
seed cracked between

the teeth of a small red
squirrel, poetry.

Thanatophobia

At night, I see the dead
in my dreams. Rotting,
stinking, they become
the stuff of root and earth.

By day, I see the dead
on the roads. Raccoons,
housecats, chunks of deer,
bloated or stiff with rigor mortis.

One day, these corpses remind me,
your mother will die. One day,
too, your father. You must burn
their lovely bodies — the skulls and palms,

even the uterus that held you.
So I pose my parents near the window,
snap their pictures, hoping
to capture their souls,

just in case some mighty god does not.

I-94 Westbound through Minnesota

On a roundbale, a red-tailed hawk,
and farther down, fields of corn,
waxy eartips bent earthward
in breeze. Behind me, a swayback
barn and a silo with glint on its head.
Later, milk cows, their flanks still
and hocked, and then the lakes —
sun-side in shimmer, set-side in oil.

So, after a lengthy season of snow-sunk
cars and frozen knees and every window
cleanly frosted over, I come to this: one
perfect July evening in northern Minnesota.
And with it, the beginnings of something
like understanding. Tired Norwegian
immigrants pushing north and north
on the hottest summer days, dirtsweat
trickling down the folds in their thick
skin, and still they keep on northward.
Until suddenly — a day like this.

The Sweet Spot

Today, rain threatens. Cool
air lofts by, twists the hands
of the maples on their wrists.
They hold on yet.

I bought the novel
I've been wanting. I can smell
the resin of its pages and feel
its starched fibers between my fingers.

Inside, the cat is surely curled
on the hardwood like a millipede
in the last spill of sun, leaving
the sofa's sweet spot for me.

How is that the world can do this?
It takes its body, sweet with autumn's
first dyings, and gives of it. I breathe in
the leak of chlorophyll, the bitter bark,
the fists of earth. My lungs fill with life
and all its glorious pain.

My Father

I. Noon to Nine

Today, my father
worked the noon to nine.
He appeared
at the screen door,
clutching a paper sack
of half-eaten lunch.
The dogs lunged
to lick the pigblood
from his boots.

He heated
the morning's coffee
in the microwave
and pulled one knee up
easily on the kitchen
chair to talk with me.
Bugs whirred toward
the ceiling light and dropped
in the crack of my book,
in his ashtray and coffee cup.
He pressed their lives out neatly
between thumbnail and wood,
snapped Barclays, one
by one, from the pack
and smoked.

Bodywearers

II. Highway Home

He steered the van down Highway 212,
gripping the wheel with only his left hand.
His thumb hitched westward
toward the swab of moonlight.
I liked that we said nothing then,
and that, for the first time this trip, he
did not smoke. His smoking hand butted out
the last at the Bird Island lights
some miles back and rested now on his
scrawny thigh. I was sleepy.
My watery reflection in the window.
The hum of the engine. And
the rearview light a mask across his eyes.

III. His Hands

He had meat-cutter's hands,
forearms roped in thick blue vein. He steadied
each Barclay in a boxy fist. Sometimes
he tweaked his boy's nose between
his fingers, and the bou breathed in
the strange blend of tar and animal blood
from his skin.

Once, at the Red Owl, he sliced
off the tip of his left pointer
with a carving knife. On the way
to the emergency room, he placed
the yellow-stained bit in the coffee cup holder,
cursing himself quietly as he drove.

With the end stitched in place, he drove
home. He knew his boy would want
to see the stitches. He right hand kept rhythm
with his steady flow of thought,
puffs and flicks, puffs and flicks.

Starting Fire in the Redwoods

Bark splits easily here.
Damp wood splints
between my thumb
and its nail as you lean
over the fire pit to nudge
a slug with a stick.

I peel back more tree,
rip to the spongy flesh.
Now the kindling
will not catch, and your
hands are stained with ash
and ink of bark. Brief
flame trembles on your jaw
and brow. The match puffs out.

I have never heard dark
set this heavily before, nor
felt air sit quite like this
on my skin. If you grow frustrated,
it does not show. Back
muscles loose, you bend
your thumb to press
the match stick hard.

The match ignites, burns,
and dies. Your face again to shadow.
I look at my fingers,
nails black as a mechanic's.

Pine Bed on the Bank of Baptism

From high on the bank
of this small creek, I see you
sunning your back on a rock
below, marking thoughts
on paper. I stand among
thick pines and lob their cones
toward you, lazy tosses
that do not reach your rock
or even splash nearby. So I look
to the treetops, the rows
of evergreens, nude
from the midriff down. We
are alone here, no hikers
for miles. Then, your hips
shift on the rock, you turn stiffly
over, catch first sight of me toeing
ungreen needles among the trunks.
A moment passes, clouds collect
near the heads of the trees, then move
on, and still you look. The creek
bubbles, the water does not reach
your toes. I listen to the soft scuttle
of brush behind me, those words
you have just written.

A Poem for the Unborn
—*for Julia*

Your mother sips decaf, orders
the soup of the day, and tosses the end

of her thick, dark braid. Your father drapes
one arm over the back of the booth and calls

for a beer. You are crowded still inside, tipping
now a bit toward birth. You jab an arm,

then an elbow, and your mother bemoans
hard bowels and swollen feet. Our baby

might have crosses eyes, your parents tell me.
The doctor thinks it's a girl, they say. Our baby

will be happy, they are certain. I know nothing
of this birthing, of this wait to push, but I

would die to know my own parents
like this — waiting, hungry, counting the days

before my arrival, the hope laid out before them,
unspoiled, what they have made.

My Mother's Ring

One afternoon in November, a month
after she laid the folded flag on her father's

coffin, my mother buys herself a ring.
Dressed in black, she prints up the showcase

with fingerpoints, choosing a square ruby
set in platinum. The jeweler eyes the gem

with his monocle, sizes her right
ring finger. He can make it fit.

A week later, Mother presses
the velvet box in my palm, the ruby

still nestled new inside. She says,
"It will be yours when I'm gone, so you

might as well have it." I accept, but
it is not a gift, it is a badge of death.

And it does not fit. I wear it one day
on my ring finger, and it spins loose.

The next day, on my pointer, it pinches
tight. So imminent death is, my mother thinks,

years or decades away. And I wear her ruby
on my finger, veined and mortal as her own.

Life

First, there's the millipede I hacked in two
this morning, its legs scrambling up the slope
of the tub despite the death of its head.

Then, my dog's stippled belly as she rolls
on her spine for a pat — the taut lip of skin
that stretches from haunch to rib
is tight as wire, inviting but one clean pluck.

And more: the upflutter of a heavy black wing,
waving in the current of vans headed north
to Nisswa or Brainerd, its body mashed
into the dotted yellow line.

All of which seems to have brought me here,
my thumb pressed against the inside
of my son's wrist as he sleeps. His bone
no bigger than a nail head.

I suppose it is perverse somehow, the way
I stare at him at night, the way I wait
for the heave of his chest, for the tender quickening
of his cheeks and lips as he suckles, his vitals.

But I have seen the drops of blood the needles
have drawn from his body. They turn him
inside out, take what my own body has sewn
and unstitch it.

The verve of his life terrifies me, the fierce
rushing of his blood. His body is too new,
too freshly part of me, who I know to be weak
and scarred.

To think, I have created this roadmap
of veins, this tiny white sheath,
this cohesive mess of flesh that balances
gently on the cusp of certain death
and terrifying, terrifying life. My baby.

Milk

After my daughter's birth,
I live with the milk. I
recline on the bed,
tuck her head in the pit
of my arm to feed.

At two months old,
she reads the cue,
widens her mouth,
purses her deep pink lips,
and tugs the nipple in.

I give myself over easily
to the pull, to the steady emptying
of my fullest breast,
and in moments she has
drawn me to sleep.

Once there, I dream of
newborns left to freeze
among the frosty reeds.
I find a blue boy in a ditch,
wailing, minutes old.

I pluck him off the ground
like a gourd, yank up
my sweater, offer my breast.
Full nipple meets new mouth,
stoppers the angry mewing.

Those cries loosen
that good and natural hold:
warm milk fills his throat,
his small soul. And
in this dream, he suckles,

how rhythmically, until he grows
fat and soft as my own daughter,
feet hot as lumps of coal
in my palm, his first dreams
a dollop of milk in drink.

Loss

When Grandad died, Death got its face.
I ran from a thousand losses: the 2 a.m.
phone call, the massive crunch of car hull
against car hull, the fetus and its fleshy slipping.

Even the small ones: a cricket leg kicking
despite the sticky web, my son's
bloodied knee, the semen coiling down
toward the gaping mouth of the toilet.

All frightening things have their stories.
The torture victims heal, form scars,
then somehow speak. Cancer is quelled,
beat down, sometimes forever. Even loss —

every body tells her own story of loss.
But Death scares us most. It
has no story, no survivors. Its face, its
horrible face — our own.

The Heron

I spot the heron first. It lifts
over the low marsh in one slow flap,
its gray arches grazing the reedtops.

You have no time to cry out,
I, no time to point. You sink
to your knees beneath its wings,
open your arms, your eyes wide.

Look there, I am thinking, his bare
knees to gravel, and there, his wings
beating sky: these are the beings I live for,
the moments I think I understand.

The Road Trip

Late March, some welcome rain,
the kids and I drive west
toward New Ulm. The baby
sleeps soundly behind me,
my young son dozes upright
in his seat. Rain slaps
steadily against the panes,
the wipers easily manage.

Miles into the trip, the chalky signs
call from just off-road: my turn-off.
I glance back at the boy.

For a moment, I let myself slip back,
crawl back under the dark covers
of childhood, still warm
from the heat of my body.

So, I steer straight instead,
dipping down the Bottom Road
toward the farm.

After all, I know what it's like:
his dense body hums with sleep. Eyes open:
scruffy horses graze beyond
the wetwood fenceposts. Eyes closed:
more of the same.

Three years old, and he trusts
the swish of the wipers,
the whir of the tire, me.
All is warm and right in the only part
of the world that matters.

Connie Colwell Miller

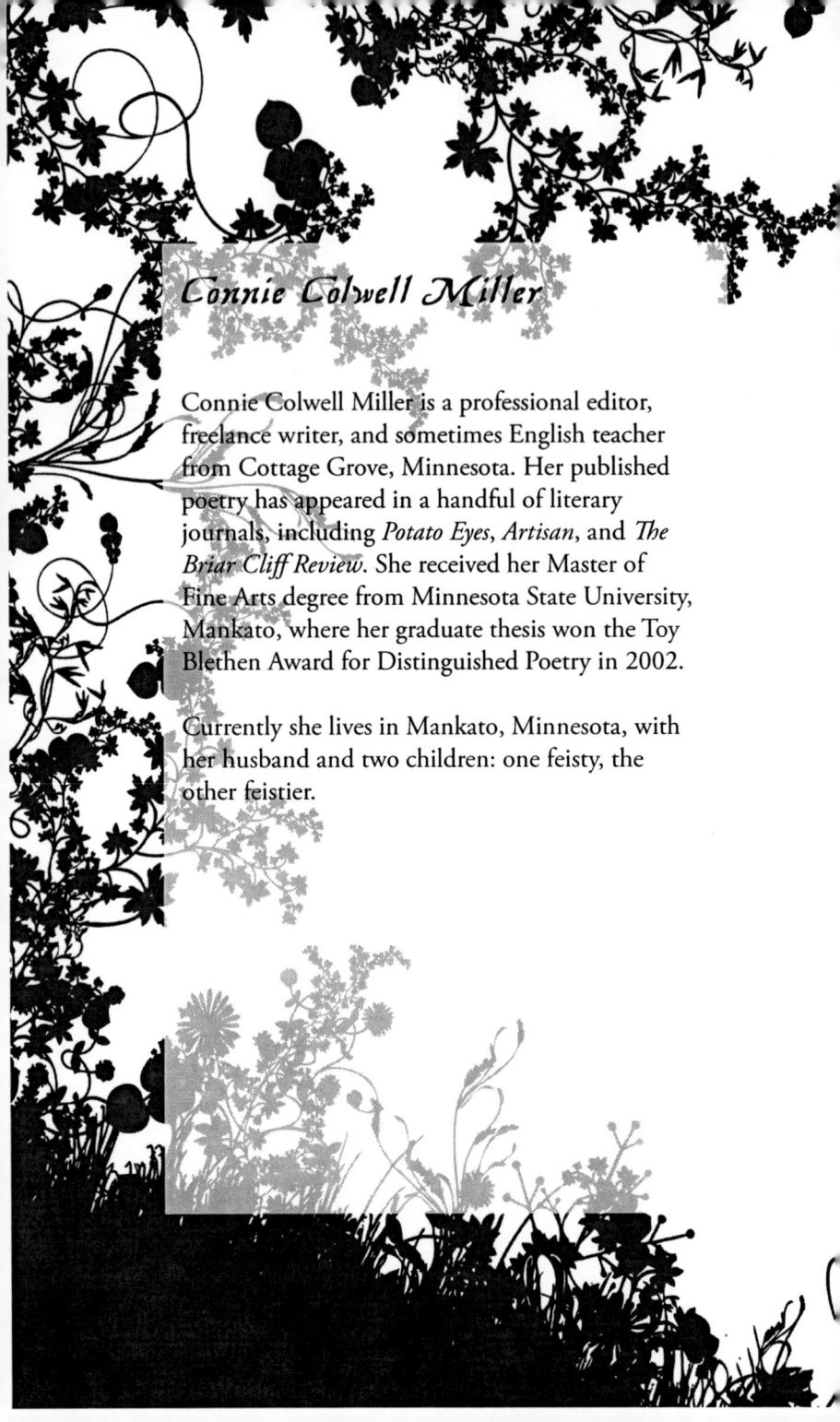

Connie Colwell Miller is a professional editor, freelance writer, and sometimes English teacher from Cottage Grove, Minnesota. Her published poetry has appeared in a handful of literary journals, including *Potato Eyes*, *Artisan*, and *The Briar Cliff Review*. She received her Master of Fine Arts degree from Minnesota State University, Mankato, where her graduate thesis won the Toy Blethen Award for Distinguished Poetry in 2002.

Currently she lives in Mankato, Minnesota, with her husband and two children: one feisty, the other feistier.

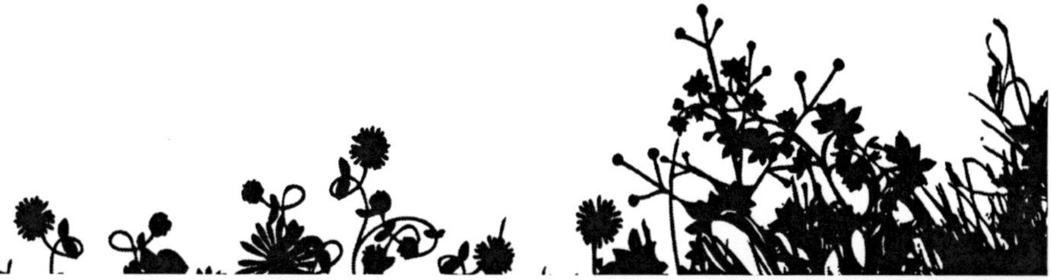

Other Sol Books Titles

Poetry Series
Pacific
  by Scott R. Welvaert

A poetic mix of *Rent* and *Romeo and Juliet*, Welvaert's *Pacific* tells the story of star-crossed lovers who set out to fulfill their dying wish: see the Pacific Ocean. They begin in Minnesota, where they meet at an AIDS clinic, journey through the Black Hills, past Devil's Tower, and to Cannon Beach, Oregon. Before reaching their destination, they must first accept their fates and the mistakes of past choices.

Prose Series
The Prostitutes of Post Office Street
  by Frank F. Carden

Post Office Street drops readers into the red-light district of Galveston, where crooked cops and down-on-their-luck prostitutes dwell. Yet, in this seedy part of town, Carden paints a picture of hope as his main characters seek to rise above the pain of broken hearts and misplaced passions, and break free from the ruts that their lives have fallen into.